LIBRARY ON WHEELS

MARY LEMIST TITCOMB AND AMERICA'S FIRST BOOKMOBILE

Sharlee Glenn

Abrams Books for Young Readers
New York

Note from the designer: The period paper elements and postage stamps incorporated into this book's design came from my personal collection. Many of the items belonged to my great-grandparents and date back to the early 1900s. The text font, Goudy Old Style, was designed by Frederic W. Goudy in 1915, and the display font, Smythe, is a contemporary take on Victorian-era typefaces designed by Vernon Adams.

Cataloging-in-Publication Data has been applied for and may be obtained from the Library of Congress.
ISBN 978-1-4197-2875-4

Printed and bound in China
10 9 8 7 6 5 4 3

Abrams Books for Young Readers are available at special discounts when purchased in quantity for premiums and promotions as well as fundraising or educational use. Special editions can also be created to specification. For details, contact specialsales@abramsbooks.com or the address below.

ABRAMS The Art of Books
195 Broadway, New York, NY 10007
abramsbooks.com

Index Page

DATE

For Mary and
all the other unsung
heroines of history

MON.
16

TUES.
17

WED.
18

THUR.
19

FRI.
20

SAT.
21

The happy person is the person who does something.
—Mary Lemist Titcomb

Mary Lemist Titcomb, 1925

MARY LEMIST TITCOMB

There are no existing photos of Mary as a young girl, but she may have looked something like this 1850s New England farm girl.

grew up wanting to do things. The problem was, people were always telling her that she couldn't. She couldn't do this, because she was too young. She couldn't do that, because she was a girl, or because her family didn't have enough money, or because it just wasn't practical. But Mary never gave up.

Titcomb family home in Farmington, New Hampshire

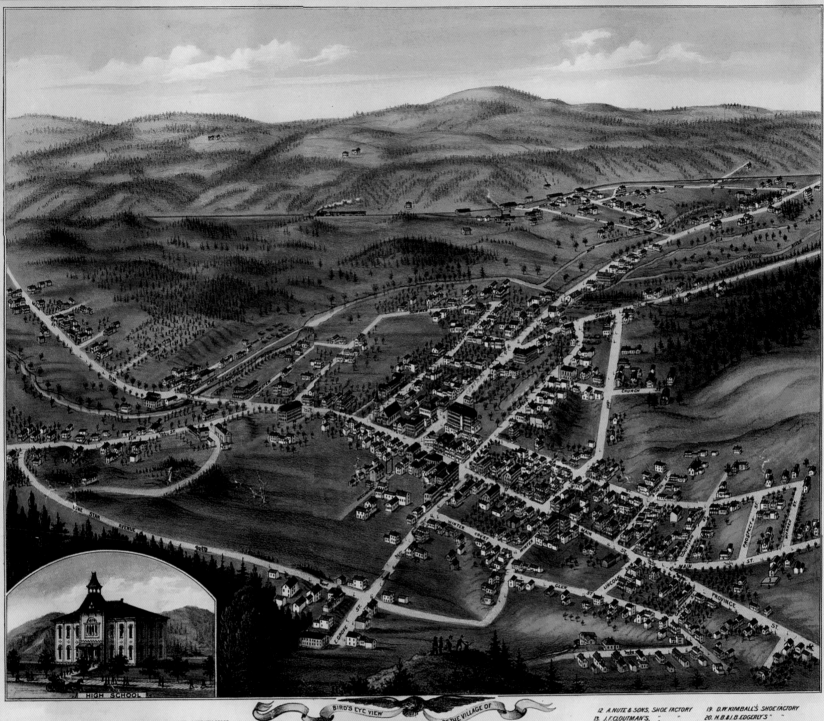

BIRD'S EYE VIEW OF THE VILLAGE OF

FARMINGTON

STRAFFORD COUNTY 1877 NEW HAMPSHIRE

1. HIGH SCHOOL	6 MECHANICS HOTEL S.VARNEY PROPR	12. A. NUTE & SONS, SHOE FACTORY	19. D.W. KIMBALL'S SHOE FACTORY
2. PUB. "	7 CONGREGATIONAL CHURCH	13. J.F. CLOUTMAN'S, "	20. H.B. & I.B. EDGERLY'S "
3. RESERVOIR	8 BAPTIST "	14. J.M. BERRY'S, "	21. W.W. HAYES SAW & PLANING MILLS
4. B. & M. R.R. DEPOT	9 ADVENT "	15. M.L. HAYES	22. L.S. FLANDERS LAST FACTORY
5. POST OFFICE	10 CEMETERY	16. GEO. A. JONES "	23. J.P. TIBBETTS CARRIAGE FACTORY
		17. E.O. CURTIS	24. EXCELSIOR MILLS
		18. J. HAYES & SONS	25. SAW

HIGH SCHOOL

Map of Farmington, New Hampshire, 1877

2

Robinson Female Seminary in Exeter, New Hampshire, where Mary attended school

Mary was born on May 16, 1852, in Farmington, New Hampshire.

Though from a poor family and in a day when academic opportunities for women were scarce, Mary was intent on getting a good educa- tion. When her family moved to Exeter, New Hampshire, so that Mary's brothers could attend the respected Phillips Exeter Academy, Mary begged for a chance to continue her schooling, too. Although it was unusual for farm girls to attend school beyond the eighth grade, Mary's parents supported the idea, and they enrolled Mary and her sister, Lydia, in the newly

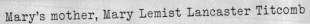

Mary's mother, Mary Lemist Lancaster Titcomb

Mary's father, George Alfred Titcomb

established Robinson Female Seminary in Exeter—a school that was meant to be the academic equivalent for girls of the Phillips Exeter Academy.

Mary loved her time at the seminary. She graduated in 1873, but continued to study French and German there as an unmatriculated student for several more years.

As Mary's brothers began leaving home to start their careers, Mary wanted to do something, too.

Students.

Graduates==Class of 1873.

Britton, Cora Ella	Newmarket.
Davis, Arrietta Marsh	Exeter.
Dow, Helen Maria	Exeter.
Harvey, Ida Belle	Newmarket.
Leavitt, Carrie Lizzie	Newmarket.
Lovering, Mary Josephine	Exeter.
Moulton, Sarah Elizabeth	Exeter.
Oakes, Mary Emma	Exeter.
Russell, Nellie Bolton	Cleveland, O.
Sanborn, Julia Augusta	East Kingston.
Sawyer, Mary Sophia	Atkinson.
Sinclair, Ida May	Exeter.
Smith, Ada Belle	Durham.
Smith, Ellen Mary	Kensington.
Titcomb, Mary Lemist	Exeter.
Wiggin, Emma Rumerell	Exeter.

Collegiate Department.

Bartlett, Ruey G.	Exeter.
Bird, Emily G.	Abeih, Syria.
Bowley, Alice E.	Exeter.

Robinson Female Seminary catalogue. Graduating class of 1873

Nursing and teaching were two of the few careers available to women at this time.

Unfortunately, aside from teaching and nursing, not many careers were open to women in the mid-nineteenth century. Her brother George became a doctor, so Mary thought she might try nursing. But she grew queasy at the mere sight of blood. And, because she felt she lacked patience, she did not think she was well suited for teaching.

One day, Mary read an article in a church bulletin about an emerging new field of work—librarianship. Mary had always loved reading. She couldn't imagine anything better than being a librarian—working all day with books and sharing those volumes with other people! That seemed the perfect life

GEORGE EUGENE TITCOMB

Mary's brother Dr. George Eugene Titcomb

for a bookworm like her. But no formal training schools for librarians existed yet; she would have to learn the profession as an apprentice.

Moving to Concord, Massachusetts, where her brother George lived, Mary began working in the library there as an unpaid assistant. She learned everything she could about librarianship—book acquisitions,

Concord Free Public Library

binding, cataloguing, classification, library administration, and more.

Mary (or Miss Titcomb, as she was now called) loved nothing more than seeing people's eyes light up when she placed the perfect book in their hands.

After completing her apprenticeship in Concord, Miss Titcomb was hired as a cat-aloguer at the Rutland Free Library in Vermont. Within a short while, she moved up into the position of chief librarian.

Miss Titcomb had found her life's work.

A woman works in a library, circa 1900

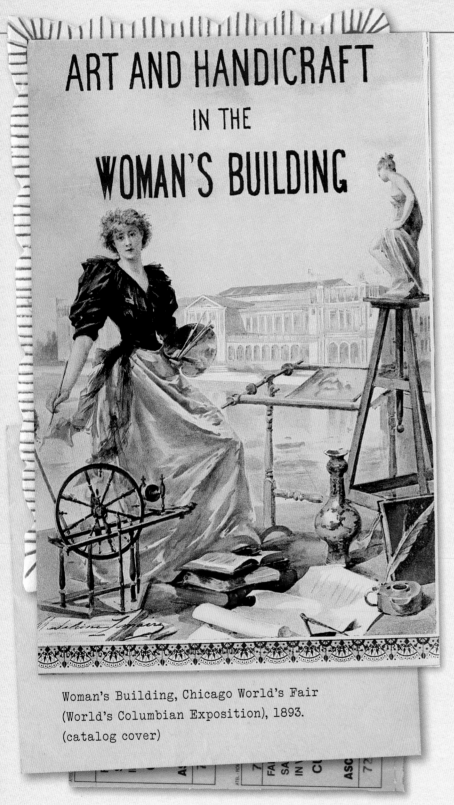

Woman's Building, Chicago World's Fair
(World's Columbian Exposition), 1893.
(catalog cover)

In 1893, Miss Titcomb submitted an application to serve as one of the librarians in the Woman's Building library at the World's Columbian Exposition, also known as the Chicago World's Fair. The whole country was abuzz with excitement over this fair, and Miss Titcomb was eager to be a part of it. Her application to serve at the Woman's Building library, however, was rejected by Mr. Melvil Dewey, the originator of the famous Dewey decimal system and president of the American Library Association (ALA).

Dewey wrote that those selected would include only "women who have been very prominent in the national association [ALA] and its work and who are very familiar with general library interests

Chicago World's Fair (World's Columbian Exposition), 1893

throughout the country." He added, "However admirable Miss Titcomb's work may have been with you [Rutland Free Library in Vermont], she has not made herself known outside."

Perhaps spurred on by Dewey's somewhat curt dismissal, Miss Titcomb, rather than give up, worked tirelessly over the next few years both to make a name for herself and to make a difference in her chosen profession.

Melvil Dewey, originator of the Dewey decimal system

Miss Titcomb aided in the establishment, organization, and improvement of dozens of libraries in Vermont and wrote articles giving advice and encouragement to librarians throughout the state. In one such bulletin, she urged librarians to "do all in your power to make the library useful. Do not make the mistake of thinking children are of no consequence. If there is any preference, let it be shown to them."

Later, in 1914, she was elected to serve as the second vice president of the ALA.

~❧◈☙~

Mary had certainly made herself known "outside" the Rutland Free Library in Vermont, and one can't help but imagine how validating this must have felt for her in light of Melvil Dewey's earlier disregard. She and Mr. Dewey were, in fact, later to become good friends. In 1910, Mr. Dewey sent Mary this postcard with a note that was very complimentary of her work.

She continually looked for ways to improve librarianship, to render it both more efficient and more far-reaching. In 1895, she was elected executive secretary of the first Vermont Library Commission and served in that capacity for the next five years. As such, she was one of the first women to hold a state office in Vermont. As executive secretary of the commission,

UNITED STATES POSTAL CARD.
ONE CENT

NOTHING BUT THE ADDRESS TO BE ON THIS SIDE.

Miss Mary L Titcomb

60   Public Library

Hagerstown   Md

ESTABLISHED 1876

American Library Association
Ex PRESIDENT, MELVIL DEWEY
Director State Library, Albany, N. Y.

Lake Placid Club N Y
28 Feb 10

Dear Miss Titcomb: Yours is the most beautiful printed report I have seen and the contents
are as attractiv as the typografy.   I congratulate you on the splendid work you are
doing and congratulate Maryland much more in
having secured you for it.   Melvil Dewey

Postcard to Mary from Melvil Dewey, 1910

Edward W. Mealey

of a local library. Once the building was complete, he began looking for a trained librarian to run it. His search took him to New England, where he found Miss Titcomb. He was later lauded for being "the instrument in the hands of God which brought Mary L. Titcomb to the people of Washington County."

Mary's friends and family thought it would be unwise for her to leave her secure position in Vermont to go by herself to rural Maryland. But Mary, always independent, was eager to take on this new challenge. In February 1901, she packed up her belongings and left for Hagerstown to assume her position as head librarian of the brand-new Washington County Free Library.

Oh, the plans she had for this library!

Meanwhile, in the thriving county seat of Hagerstown, Maryland, a forward-thinking citizen by the name of Edward W. Mealey decided that Washington County needed a library. Mr. Mealey had been educated at Harvard University and had observed firsthand the growth of the library movement in New England. So he set about raising funds for the construction

14

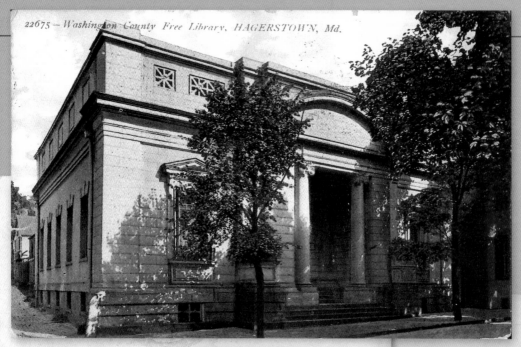

22675 – Washington County Free Library, HAGERSTOWN, Md.

The Washington County
Free Library

Public Square – 7

Hagerstown, Maryland, public square, 1905

STORY

of the

WASHINGTON COUNTY FREE LIBRARY

Mary L. Titcomb

WRITTEN BY

MARY LEMIST TITCOMB, *Librarian 1901-1931*

at the request of

The Board of Directors of the Chamber
of Commerce, Hagerstown, Maryland

———

Foreword By
COL. JOSEPH C. BYRON
*President of the Board of Trustees
of the Library*

Title page (signed by Mary) of *Story of the Washington County Free Library* by Mary Lemist Titcomb with a foreword by Col. Joseph C. Byron

Public lending libraries were still a fairly new idea in America, and county libraries that served not only the residents of a particular town or city, but an entire county sometimes hundreds of square miles large, were almost unheard of. In fact, the Washington County Free Library was only the second county-wide library in the nation. The first, the Brumback Library, located in Van Wert, Ohio, had opened its doors only a few months earlier.

There were those who thought the whole venture would be a failure. They felt that the county's farmers and working people had no time or use for books. Others were angry that the library's board of directors had brought in an outsider to run the operation. As Col. Joseph C. Byron, president of the board, later wrote in the foreword to *Story of the Washington County Free Library*, "People were not educated up to the idea of a public library. Libraries were for the idle and the rich. It remained for Miss Titcomb to show us that libraries are intended for the middle class of people, the working man and woman and children particularly."

Once again, Miss Titcomb ignored the naysayers and went to work.

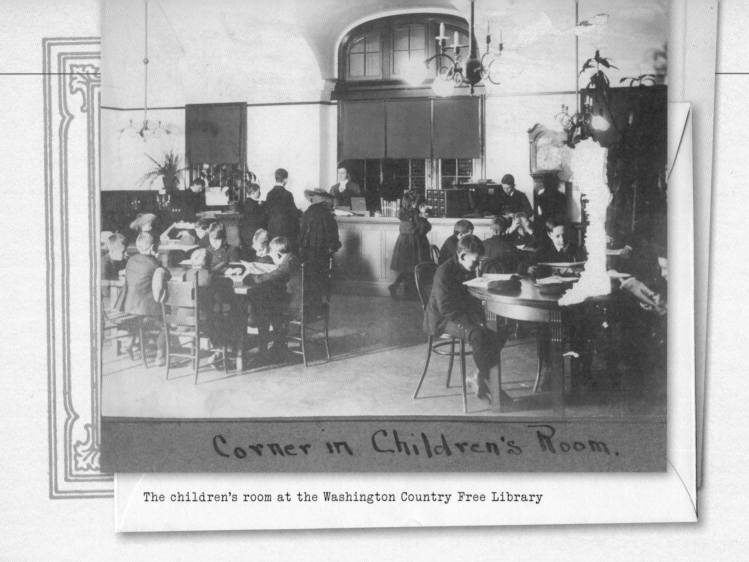

Corner in Children's Room.

The children's room at the Washington Country Free Library

When the Washington County Free Library opened its doors on

August 27, 1901, the citizens of Hagerstown showed up in throngs, and, as Miss Titcomb later wrote, "any secret and lingering doubts as to the acceptance of the institution . . . were dispelled once and for all." Miss Titcomb liked to tell about how one "scrubwoman" left the library that day, a book wrapped carefully in her apron, exclaiming, "It's a great day when poor folks like us can take home such handsome books."

The library was an undisputed success. Miss Titcomb later wrote that the library "at once established itself as an educational, recreational and democratizing influence in the community, bringing all classes of people to it."

But Miss Titcomb knew that the library was not yet achieving its full purpose. It had been established for *all* the residents of Washington County, but over half of them—some 25,000 people—lived far from town, on farms scattered across nearly 500 square miles. How to get the library's books to them?

Miss Titcomb was determined that *everyone* should have access to the library—not just adults, not just the rich or educated, not just those who lived in town. She was absolutely unwavering in her dedication to this vision.

Story hour, Brownsville, Washington County, Maryland

First, she opened a children's room in the library—one of the first in the nation.

She also made sure that all the outlying village schools had a good rotating supply of books and pictures from the library. Then she started a storytelling hour in remote areas to get the country children excited about books and reading.

19

MILL OFFICE AT WEST BEAVER CREEK

Book deposit box at the West Beaver Creek mill office, Washington County, Maryland

Next, she set up book deposit stations throughout the county.

These served as small branch libraries where people could check out books, then return the ones they had already read. As Miss Titcomb wrote: "Since its doors were opened in 1901, it has been the unceasing effort of the management to make the library as vital a thing in the country as in the town. To this end, deposit stations (seventy-five in number) have been scattered over its territory, placed in the country store, the post office, the creameries, at the tollgates, or, if nothing better offered, in some private houses."

As successful as the book deposit stations were, they still weren't serving all the county's residents—especially those who lived on backcountry farms, far up in the

Book deposit box in Green Springs Furnace, Washington County, Maryland

A difficult journey

Remote areas of Washington County, Maryland, where Mary wanted to bring books to the residents

A mountain road

foothills of the Blue Ridge and Cumberland mountains. But Miss Titcomb didn't give up. In 1905, she had her most revolutionary idea of all—a horse-drawn "book wagon." Why not fit a wagon with shelves and take the library to the people? she thought. "The book goes to the man. We do not wait for the man to come to the book."

Again, the naysayers were quick to voice their objections. It seemed an outlandish proposition to them. A wagon to take books to every farmhouse in the county? Farmers didn't have time to read books! And who was going to pay for this new contraption, anyway?

"Here indeed [we] embarked upon an uncharted sea," admitted Miss Titcomb. But she was not deterred. She met with several wagonmakers and came up with a design. Then she presented her idea to the board of trustees at the library. They scratched their heads. It sounded like a crazy plan. But by now, the board had learned that when Miss Titcomb decided to do something, she did it.

They granted their approval.

In just four short years since her arrival, Miss Titcomb had won the hearts and gained the admiration of the library board and the people of Hagerstown.

Miss Titcomb, 1925

A PEN SKETCH OF HAGERSTOWN'S LIBRARIAN

Something about the Career and Home Life of Miss Mary Lemist Titcomb,

Who made a Local Institution Famous.

By FLORA B. ZEIGLER

The World's Work for February 1913 and other magazines have given well merited publicity to the Washington County Free Library, with its unique feature, a library wagon (now an automobile) literally peddling notions-information, to the rural folk. But the Library and wagon are familiar to many, who scarcely know the name of the little woman whose head and heart furnished the inspirational energy that keeps the work in the honor list of new and exceptional effort. When Miss Titcomb was asked to tell something of herself, she replied, as do most people who have done things, "there is nothing to tell". Even the persistency of the interviewer secured only a few facts on which to build this sketch.

HER GIRLHOOD DAYS

Mary Lemist Titcomb was born in Farmington, N. H., but spent her girlhood in the school town of Exeter. She is one of two daughters and has four brothers. In those days the public schools were not in high favor and these girls had the advantage of being taught at home by the mother. Later Miss Titcomb graduated from the Robinson Female Seminary.

One who knew her well says she was a shy, timid girl, easily frightened into being almost panicky, when forced into speech and action by the even greater timidity of her sister. Like many New England homes this one had a literary and educational atmosphere, intensified, no doubt, by the college spirit of the brothers, who were students at the Philips Exeter Academy and others who must have found the wholesome, fun-loving Mary Titcomb good company, despite her "shyness'.

Miss Titcomb seems to have had no definite thought of work as a career, but when the family was broken up by the death of the father and the marriage of her brothers, she wanted "something to do".

TAKES UP LIBRARY WORK

Having a physician brother, her first thoughts were of nursing, but she promptly recognized her unfitness for that vocation. An article in a church paper called her attention to "Library Work an Opening for Women". Books, and work among them appealed to her as very congenial, and at once she decided to enter the comparatively new field. Training schools for librarians were then unknown and Miss Tit-

comb became an unpaid assistant in the Library of Concord, Mass. Her next position was as cataloguer for the Free Library of Rutland, Vt., and later she was made librarian in chief. For a number of years Miss Titcomb was secretary for the Vermont Library Commission, she and Miss Louise Bartlett having the distinction of being the first women to hold state offices in Vermont.

ORGANIZED MANY LIBRARIES

For twelve years Miss Titcomb was organizer of libraries and re-organizer of those that needed to be put on a new footing.

While at Rutland, Miss Titcomb was granted permission to catalogue the library of Vermont diocese in the residence of Bishop Hall in Burlington.

These experiences developed the resourcefulness and the versitility of idea and plan characterizing her work today.

HER WORK IN HAGERSTOWN

When our Library was opened thirteen years ago in charge of Miss Titcomb many of us thought of it as only a place to get books, but the Librarian made it clear that giving out books to those who came for them was a small part of her business. She was to popularize the Library and create a demand for its wares, which she proceeded to prove were as varied as the goods in a department store. The building became a meeting place for committees and organizations looking toward civic, educational and moral betterment, while the Librarian identified herself with community interests, keeping step with every forward movement, while many times her thought was in advance of it. Steadily Miss Titcomb has won her way among us, disarming criticism, overcoming prejudice, strengthening her influence and all the time justifying her appointment by bringing things to pass with energetic efficiency.

HER HOME LIFE

It is in her home that Miss Titcomb, the woman, is seen to the best advantage. The house is an attractive modern one, built after her own plan. Running the full width of the front is a living room, the envy of all who see it. At one end is a large circular window; at the other double windows open on the veranda. In the center is a wide fire place with cozy seats by the "Ingle-side". Book shelves are overhead

and a little cupboard, holding the kettle, the tea-caddy and pretty china, used in serving the "cup that cheers."

In this room one afternoon several callers happened to meet. Without, the air was cold and blustery; within, a glowing fire, the fragrance of flowers and the hum of conversation created a delightful atmosphere. Among the visitors was one who knew Miss Titcomb only as the professional librarian, somewhat austere, with a suggestion of frost in her manner, credited to the "New England temperament."

It was interesting to note signs of capitulation to the personality of the woman.

The hostess was most gracious, most charming. She wore a soft gray silk and a dainty slipper was visible. The hostile one saw it, saw too—could she believe it? —the feminine frivolity, a jeweled buckle. She heard too, the little woman discussing "Spring Fashions", vivaciously, knowingly, for Miss Titcomb is no mean authority on style and her dress, like her work, is always up-to-date.

MAKES DRESSES AND COOKS

Unblushingly she confessed to "making many of her own things." Later, she showed a room, furnished with a sewing machine, a work table, a gas iron for pressing and a figure for fitting and draping. There the librarian becomes dressmaker and finds rest in change of work.

The capitulation had begun.

Further conversation developed that Miss Titcomb really enjoyed housekeeping, was even fond of cooking.

The capitulation progressed.

HER LOVE OF CHILDREN

Miss Titcomb's love of children and her understanding and appreciation of their whims and caprices are well known. She referred to a recent visit to Washington as fine, "because she had with her a little maiden of five whose unrestrained delight in everything was contagious," and whose ceaseless questions kept her in a mild state of excitement, wondering "what next".

The capitulation was complete.

INTENSELY WOMANLY

These things indicate that Miss Titcomb is intensely womanly as well as professionally competent, and that her womanliness

[Continued on page 8]

"To Miss Titcomb alone belongs the credit of the upbuilding of the Library. Her personality has been stamped upon it. She has never gone backward. She has not even faltered," wrote Col. Joseph C. Byron, the president of the library's board of trustees. And a local newspaper article declared that "steadily Miss Titcomb has won her way among us, disarming criticism, overcoming prejudice, strengthening her influence."

"The library refuses to stand still," wrote Col. Joseph C. Byron in 1931, "and the reason is Miss Titcomb. To attempt to write the history of the Washington County Free Library without devoting some time to Miss Titcomb would be like trying to write the history of the Ark without mentioning Noah."

Col. Joseph C. Byron, president of the Washington County Free Library's board of trustees

Having gained the approval of the library board, Miss Titcomb and the wagonmakers went to work. The "book wagon" had long shelves built on each side covered by doors that opened outward. The shelves could hold about two hundred books, and the main body of the wagon could

Typical grocer's cart of the time

also carry several large cases of books for the deposit stations along the route.

According to Miss Titcomb, the horse-drawn conveyance looked like "a cross between a grocer's delivery wagon and the tin peddler's cart of bygone New England days."

When Miss Titcomb first saw the finished book wagon, she worried that it looked too much like a laundry truck or a peddler's wagon, so she instructed the builder to paint the whole thing a dig-nified black and to print WASHINGTON COUNTY FREE LIBRARY on the sides in plain lettering, with no scrolls or fuss. The painter followed these directions very well. Maybe too well, for when the book wagon approached a farmhouse on one of its first trips into the countryside, the driver heard a nervous voice call out: "Yer needn't stop here. We ain't got no use for the dead wagon here!" After that, Miss Titcomb wasted no time in painting the book wagon's wheels and door panels a bright, cheery red to avoid any confusion with a hearse!

The book wagon made its maiden voyage in April 1905. Although Miss Titcomb rode along whenever she could, she still had her duties to fulfill back at the main library, so Mr. Joshua Thomas, the library janitor, was enlisted to be the driver. The wagon was pulled by a pair of dapper horses named Black Beauty and Dandy.

LIBRARY WAGON.

America's first book wagon, pulled by Black Beauty and Dandy, 1905

Joshua Thomas helps children select books from the new book wagon.

Mr. Thomas had grown up in Washington County and was a veteran of the Civil War. After the war, he'd made a living by riding through the country-side buying produce, eggs, and butter to sell in the market in Hagerstown. "In this way," wrote Miss Titcomb, "he learned every road and byway in the County and was known by all the residents, un-consciously being prepared for this later undertaking." To Miss Titcomb's way of thinking, the human element was a crit-ical part of the book-wagon experience, and Mr. Thomas related well to people, especially the farmers. And Mr. Thomas obviously loved his job. On the 1910 U.S. census, he listed his occupation as "Book Missionary."

The book wagon (or "Book Contraption,"

The Hixon farmhouse, typical of the places where the book wagon would have stopped

as some of the locals called it) made thirty-one trips in the first six months and lent out over a thousand books.

For the next five years, the book wagon faithfully traveled the roads of Washington County, carrying volumes to the outlying villages and farms. Children who had never owned a book in their lives suddenly could borrow dozens at a time!

"The sound of the approaching book wagon brings the family from the fields, the barns, and the house." wrote Miss Titcomb. "It is an important day when the Washington County book wagon stops at

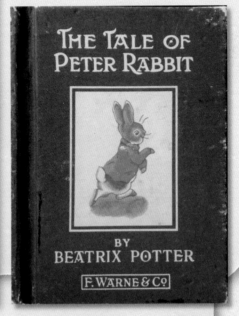

Some of the volumes that children might have borrowed from the first book wagon: *Little Women* (published in 1868), *The Wonderful Wizard of Oz* (published in 1900), and *The Tale of Peter Rabbit* (published in 1902).

the farm, because the family is allowed to borrow as many as thirty books at a time, from scientific treatises on farming, for father, to colored picture books, for baby."

The book wagon had exceeded everyone's expectations.

Then, in the fall of 1910, disaster struck. The book wagon was hit by a train while crossing the Norfolk and Western Railway tracks at St. James. Fortunately, the horses were not injured, and Mr. Thomas escaped with only minor bruises. The book wagon, however, was completely destroyed, along with all its books. For a while, it looked as if that might be the end of this bold new experiment.

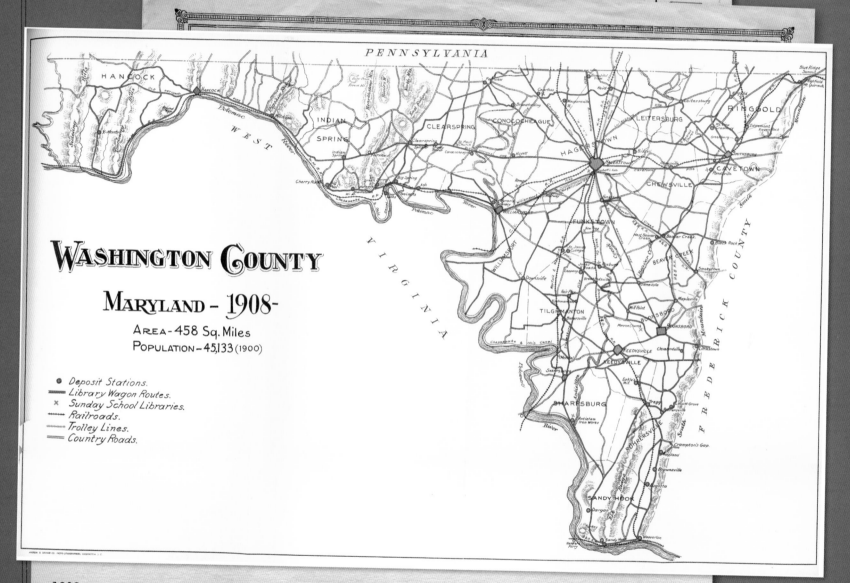

1908 map of Washington County showing deposit stations and book wagon routes

The second book wagon—a motorized International
Harvester Auto Wagon, 1912

But Miss Titcomb didn't give up. She secured funds for a new wagon from a longtime member of the library board who had watched her do what so many had said couldn't be done. With full confidence in Miss Titcomb and her dream, this board member, Mr. William Kealhofer, stepped forward with a donation of $2,500 for the purchase of a new book wagon. The "horseless carriage" was beginning to replace the horse and buggy, and Miss Titcomb and the board decided to buy a motorized vehicle this time—a customized International Harvester Auto Wagon that could hold three hundred books.

As Mr. Thomas did not know how to operate a motorcar, Miss Titcomb and the board hired a driver and put Miss

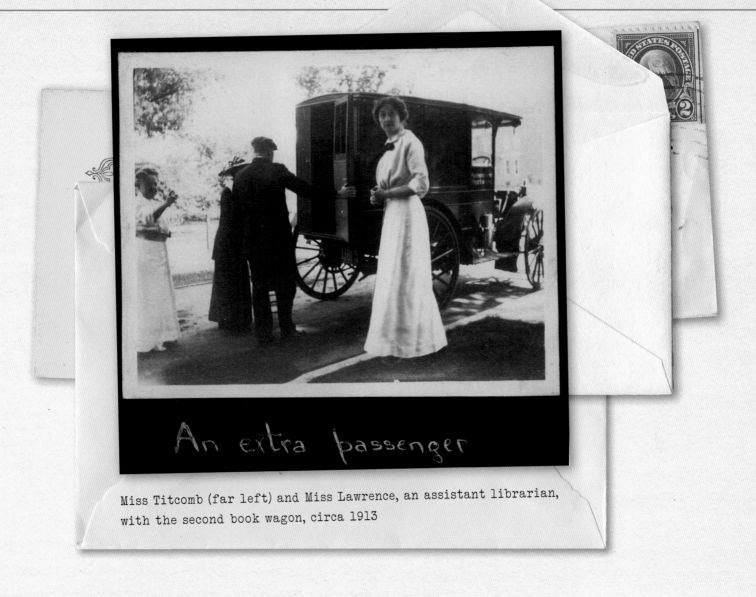

An extra passenger

Miss Titcomb (far left) and Miss Lawrence, an assistant librarian, with the second book wagon, circa 1913

Nellie Chrissinger, an assistant librarian, in charge of the new book wagon. Miss Chrissinger would spend the next twenty-four years traveling throughout Washington County in the "wagon."

She later said, "The library is my whole life—and the book wagon is the real joy in that life."

With the new truck, the scope of the library's outreach expanded. New routes were added, and the book truck was able to cover each route three times a year. Just

Miss Chrissinger with children, second book wagon, 1912–1916

WPA bookmobile, North Carolina Library Commission, 1937

Rockingham County, North Carolina, bookmobile, circa 1930

three years later, an even larger vehicle was needed. The new book wagon could carry five hundred books and up to six cases for the deposit stations and schools.

It was roomy enough to seat Miss Chrissinger, the driver, and one additional passenger. That extra seat was rarely empty, because, by this time, the book wagon was becoming quite famous. Politicians, journalists, librarians, and many other interested people came from all over the country to ride along and observe, firsthand, the magic of America's first traveling library.

Soon, book wagons began appearing in other parts of the country—Indiana, Minnesota, Delaware, Illinois—and by 1922, the book wagon idea had received widespread support, thanks largely to the efforts of Miss Titcomb, who wrote and lectured about it extensively.

The bookmobile had been born.

This painting (circa 1920s) was painted by G. A. Rudy, a contemporary of Miss Titcomb. It hangs in the Washington County Library.

And, thanks to Mary Lemist Titcomb, the determined girl who never gave up, America was changed forever.

Washington County
Bookmobiles
Through the Years

And by the 1960s, there were nearly two thousand bookmobiles in the United States bringing books to over fifty million people in rural communities.

LIBRARY WAGON.

1905
The original book wagon

1912,
first
motorized
bookmobile

1920s
bookmobile,
with Miss
Chrissinger

1930s
bookmobile

1940s
bookmobile

1950s
bookmobile

2016
bookmobile

The Library refuses to stand still, and the reason is Miss Titcomb.
—Col. Joseph C. Byron

Author's Note

Early in 2014, I was doing research for a book on our nation's first library when I ran across an obscure reference to a woman named Mary Lemist Titcomb who was credited with the invention of the bookmobile in America. A woman had invented the bookmobile? I was immediately intrigued. Growing up as a book-loving child in rural Utah in the 1960s and '70s, I developed a strong emotional connection to the bookmobile. My father died in a mining accident when I was five, leaving my mother with seven children to raise on her own. We didn't have much money or many opportunities, but every two weeks the bookmobile brought the universe to me.

So the focus of my research quickly shifted to Mary Lemist Titcomb and her bookmobile. And thus began my remarkable journey. I learned that, while there had been a few mule-drawn wagons carrying books from place to place in nineteenth-century England, Mary was the first to conceive of and implement a formalized plan for rural distribution of books by use of a book wagon in the United States. The more I uncovered in my research, the more excited I became. It wasn't easy to find a lot of information about Mary, and what I found was often inaccurate. For example, most of the secondary accounts I read listed her birth year as 1857, but as I dug deeper into birth records and other primary documents, I discovered that she was actually born in 1852. Several accounts also had her dying in January 1932, but when a great-niece of Mary's found a letter in Mary's own hand dated April 19, 1932, we knew that that couldn't be true! Eventually, we were able to verify her date of death as June 5, 1932. I felt a bit like a detective as I combed through birth and death records, census reports, school catalogues,

old newspapers, ship passenger lists, personal letters, and other historical documents, trying to piece together a coherent portrait of this remarkable but hitherto unheralded woman. Along the way, I discovered a whole host of intriguing tidbits about her life. It was fascinating work and great fun!

Mary never married and had no children, but I was able to find a great-niece of hers living in Oregon who has been tremendously helpful. The two of us have spoken on the phone, corresponded, and shared information and documents like gleeful genealogists. This great-niece provided me with family histories and copies of several of Mary's personal letters. Later, I tracked down a great-grandnephew of Mary's living in Vermont who likewise proved to be a treasure trove, sharing with me original family photographs, newspaper clippings, and family letters.

Early on in my research, I read that Mary was buried in the Sleepy Hollow Cemetery in Concord, Massachusetts. I had fallen in love with that particular cemetery several years earlier when I made a pilgrimage there with my daughter after learning that my favorite childhood writer, Louisa May Alcott, the author of *Little Women*, was buried there. It was Louisa May Alcott, along with her endearing and enduring character Jo March, who first lit in me the desire to be a writer. I contacted the supervisor of the cemetery, Tish Hopkins, who confirmed that Mary Lemist Titcomb was, indeed, buried there—but in an unmarked grave. I was shocked. This extraordinary woman who had contributed so much to American culture had no headstone?

Since Mary had no direct descendants, and since she'd outlived

Author and daughter with newly installed headstone for Mary Lemist Titcomb. Sleepy Hollow Cemetery, Concord, Massachusetts, May 16, 2015.

headstones for both Mary and Lydia. She put me in contact with Kevin Plodzik, president of the nonprofit Friends of Sleepy Hollow Cemetery, and together we decided that if I could raise the funds for Lydia's headstone, the Friends of Sleepy Hollow would cover the expense for Mary's stone and a memorial service. Thanks to the quick and generous response of book lovers across the globe (many of whom, like me, had been personally affected by the bookmobile), the necessary money was raised in a matter of weeks. And the rest, as they say, is history. Or, in this case, *her*-story.

On May 16, 2015, I flew to Concord, Massachusetts, to speak at the unveiling of the headstones. I felt as if I were standing on hallowed ground, there in Sleepy Hollow Cemetery, overlooking not only Mary's grave, but also the cemetery's famed Authors Ridge, where lay, among other such literary notables as Nathaniel Hawthorne and Ralph Waldo Emerson, my childhood role model, Louisa May Alcott. It seemed to me an utterly beautiful and poetic stroke of serendipity that Mary Lemist Titcomb, the mother of the bookmobile whose story I was writing, was buried a mere stone's toss from Louisa May Alcott, the person who had inspired me to write books in the first place.

And so Mary now has not only a headstone, but also a book. It is one of the great honors of my life to be able to present to you, the reader, an account of the life and accomplishments of this remarkable woman. So many people told Mary that she couldn't do what she did—because she was a girl, because her family was poor, because it was too hard, because it was impractical. But Mary did it anyway. If, as Mary claimed in a newspaper interview in 1923, "the happy person is the person who does something," then Mary was among the happiest of all people.

Mary Lemist Titcomb, may you and your work never again be forgotten.

both her parents and most of her siblings, apparently there was no one to ensure that she'd be memorialized after she died. She had lived most of her adult life in Hagerstown, Maryland, but upon her death, she was cremated and her remains sent to Concord to be interred in the family plot. I learned that Mary's sister, Lydia Folsom Titcomb Howell, was also buried there, right next to Mary—also in an unmarked grave. I told Tish I wanted to raise the money for

The bookmobile that served the author's little farming community in Utah when she was growing up in the 1960s and 1970s

Notes

(Full citations listed in **Select Bibliography**)

Page iv: "The happy person": From an article ("Dramatic Institute Opens") that appeared in Hagerstown, Maryland's daily newspaper, the *Morning Herald*, January 11, 1923.

Page 3: "Mary was born on": While some secondary sources list Mary's birth year as 1857, she was actually born in 1852, as verified by official birth records and census reports (see Selected Bibliography). At some point, Mary herself apparently shaved five years off her age, perhaps so that she could continue doing the work she so loved without outside pressure to retire due to age. As it was, Mary maintained an active schedule as head librarian of the Washington County Free Library until just a few months before her death at age eighty-one.

Page 3: "Although it was unusual": Mary's mother, Mary Elizabeth Lancaster Titcomb, was remarkably well educated for a nineteenth-century farm wife. As a child, she was taught Greek and Latin by an elderly uncle and was sent to school at New Hampshire's Gilmanton Academy. Mary (her daughter) wrote of her: "In a very busy life with many children and the old people of Father's side to care for, she always found time for books and music and her garden. The older I grow, the more I realize how remarkable she was." Titcomb, "Regarding Mary L. Titcomb," letter to a niece or nephew.

Pages 4–5: "Robinson Female Seminary in Exeter": The founder of the seminary, William Robinson, was a native of Exeter who was orphaned as a child but went on to do very well for himself. At his death in 1866, he left a large portion of his money to the town of Exeter for the establishment of an academy for girls. Robinson's will stated: ". . . there is altogether too much partaking of the fancy in the educations that females obtain, and I would most respectfully suggest such a course of instruction as will tend to make female scholars equal . . . [and] enable them to compete, and successfully too, with their brothers throughout the world." The will specified that the money be used only for the education of females, with preference given to the "poor and the orphan." From "Trustees of the Robinson Fund."

Pages 10–11: "Dewey wrote that those selected": Wadsworth and Wiegand, *Right Here I See My Own Books*, 96.

Page 12: "do all in your power": "Suggestions to the Librarian of a Small Library," *First Biennial Report of the Board of Library Commissioners of Vermont, 1895–96.*

Page 14: "the instrument in the hands of God": Byron, foreword to *Story of the Washington County Free Library.*

Page 17: "The first, the Brumback Library": Gilliland, ed., *History of Van Wert County, Ohio*, 253.

Page 17: "People were not educated": Byron, foreword to *The Washington County Free Library.*

Page 18: "any secret and lingering": Titcomb and Holzapfel, *The Washington County Free Library*, 9.

Page 18: "It's a great day": Ibid., 9.

Page 19: "Miss Titcomb later wrote": Ibid., 10.

Page 20: "Since its doors were opened": Titcomb, "A County Library," 4.

Page 22: "The book goes to the man": Titcomb, ibid., 6.

Page 23: "Here indeed [we] embarked": Titcomb and Holzapfel, *The Washington County Free Library*, 10.

Page 25: "To Miss Titcomb alone": Byron, foreword to *The Washington County Free Library*.

Page 25: "steadily Miss Titcomb has won": Zeigler, "A Pen Sketch," 5.

Page 25: "The library refuses to stand still": Byron, foreword to *The Washington County Free Library*.

Page 26: "a cross between a grocer's": Titcomb and Holzapfel, *The Washington County Free Library*, 14.

Page 26: "Yer needn't stop here": Titcomb, "On the Trail of the Book Wagon," 10.

Page 26: "After that, Miss Titcomb": Titcomb, "On the Trail of the Book Wagon," 10.

Page 26: "The Wagon was pulled": According to a handwritten note penciled on a photograph labeled THE FIRST BOOK WAGON in the archives of the Western Maryland Regional Library, the horses that pulled the original book wagon were named Dandy and Black Beauty (www.whilbr.org; note under "The First Book Wagon" photo). In a 1949 interview, however, E. A. Corderman, the owner of the livery stable that rented out the horses for the first book wagon, stated that the horses were actually named Bill and Maude. See "Operator of First Bookmobile Here Tells of Early Activities," 32.

Page 28: "'In this way,' wrote Miss Titcomb": Titcomb and Holzapfel. *The Washington County Free Library*, 14.

Page 29: "The sound of the approaching": Titcomb and Mason, *Book Wagons*, 2.

Page 32: "With full confidence": Titcomb and Holzapfel, 14.

Page 33: "The library is my whole life": "Former Local Librarian Dies," the *Morning Herald*, July 8, 1955.

Page 35: "Soon book wagons began appearing": Titcomb and Mason, *Book Wagons*, 8–9. In 1922, Miss Titcomb wrote with great pride about a librarian in Delaware, Miss Hopkins, who had followed her lead: "In Sussex County, Delaware, there is a librarian who has driven a horse and buggy, and now a car, for the past nine years . . . She places a case of books on the rear seat, and away she goes to the country, gladdening the hearts of the children, interesting the young folks, and occasionally finding a farmer and his wife who are not too sleepy to read a bit after the day's work is done. She has stayed overnight with her people, helped the farmer's wife wipe the dishes at ten o'clock and has risen with her at three-thirty a.m. for the day's work. A year or so ago, she introduced an easy method of canning string-beans that delighted the practical hearts of the housewives. Miss Hopkins, herself, wrote: 'Every trip confirms my faith in the book wagon. It preaches no sermons, but its books silently and delightfully influence character and make people think . . . Oh, for millions of dollars to send the traveling libraries over all the roads of the country!'" Titcomb and Mason, *Book Wagons*, 10.

Page 36: "And by the 1960s": Institute of Museum and Library Services. www.imls.gov.

Select Bibliography

Books

Byron, Joseph C. "Foreword," in *Story of the Washington County Free Library*, by Mary Lemist Titcomb. Hagerstown, MD: n.p., 1931.

Gilliland, Thaddeus, ed. *History of Van Wert County, Ohio*. Chicago: Richmond and Arnold, 1906.

Titcomb, Mary Lemist. *Story of the Washington County Free Library, 1901–1931*. Hagerstown, MD: n.p., 1931.

"Titcomb, Mary Lemist." In *Woman's Who's Who of America: A Biographical Dictionary of Contemporary Women of the United States and Canada, 1914–1915*. Edited by John William Leonard. New York: The American Commonwealth Co., 1915.

Titcomb, Gilbert Merrill. *Descendants of William Titcomb of Newbury, Mass., 1635*. Ann Arbor, MI: Edwards Brothers, 1969.

Titcomb, Mary Lemist, and Mary Frank Mason. *Book Wagons; the County Library with Rural Book Delivery*. Chicago: American Library Association, 1922.

Titcomb, Mary Lemist, and Mary Louise Holzapfel. *The Washington County Free Library, 1901–1951*. (Being a reissue of the *Story of the Washington County Free Library*). (Hagerstown, MD: n.p., 1951.

Wadsworth, Sarah, and Wayne A. Wiegand. *Right Here I See My Own Books: The Woman's Building at the World's Columbian Exposition*. Amherst: University of Massachusetts, 2012.

Interview

Beatty, Greata. Telephone interview by Sharlee Glenn, April 10, 2014. (Greata is the great-niece of Mary Lemist Titcomb and the granddaughter of Mary's brother John Wheelock Titcomb).

Journal Articles

Craig, Jill. "The First Bookmobile." *Catoctin History, no. 10* (Spring/Summer 2008), 12–20.

"Robinson Female Seminary" in *The American Journal of Education*, edited by Henry Barnard, 439–44. Vol. 24. Hartford, CT: Office of American Journal of Education, 1873.

Titcomb, Mary L. "Suggestions to the Librarian of a Small Library." *First Biennial Report of the Board of Library Commissioners of Vermont, 1895–96*. Burlington, VT: Burlington Free Press Association, Printers, 1896.

Letters

Howell, Lilla T. to Jonathan "Jack" Titcomb. 326 Summit Avenue, Hagerstown, MD. January 9, 1930. Handwritten letter.

Titcomb, Mary. "AM." Handwritten letter to Margaret Titcomb, March 28 [no year indicated].

Titcomb, Mary "Aunt Minnie" L. Handwritten letter to Jonathan "Jack" Titcomb. April 19, 1932.

——. Typed letter to niece, Margaret. Undated.

Titcomb, Mary Elizabeth Lancaster. "My Dear Eugene." Letter to George Eugene Titcomb. February 22, 1889.

Titcomb, Mary Lemist. "Regarding Mary L. Titcomb." Letter to a niece or nephew. March 30, 193_ [date illegible].

Newspaper Articles

"Circulating Library Is Housed in an Automobile." *Anaconda Standard*, Anaconda, MT, June 1, 1913.

"Dramatic Institute Opens with a Big Enrollment." *Morning Herald*, Hagerstown, MD, January 11, 1923.

"Former Local Librarian Dies." *Morning Herald*, Hagerstown, MD, July 8, 1955.

"Library Book Van Smashed in a Railroad Wreck." *Daily Mail*, Hagerstown, MD, August 25, 1910.

"Miss Titcomb, Library Head, Dies at Home." *Daily Mail*, Hagerstown, MD, June 6, 1932.

"Miss Titcomb's Appointment." *The Daily Herald*, Delphos, OH, February 27, 1901.

"Operator of First Bookmobile Here Tells of Early Activities." *Daily Mail*, Hagerstown, MD, February 25, 1949.

"Organizer of First County Library Here, Miss Mary Lemist Titcomb, Hagerstown, Attends Conference in Town, Is Founder of Rural System." *Gettysburg Times*, Gettysburg, PA, April 7 1932.

Zeigler, Flora B. "A Pen Sketch of Hagerstown's Librarian: Something about the Career and Home Life of Miss Mary Lemist Titcomb, Who Made a Local Institution Famous." *The Builder*, Hagerstown, MD, November 15, 1913.

Online Collections/Websites

"The Bookmobile Collection." WHILBR-Bookmobile. Western Maryland Regional Library: Western Maryland's Historical Library, www.whilbr.org/bookmobile/index.aspx (accessed April 21, 2014–January 23, 2017).

Institute of Museum and Library Services. www.imls.gov (accessed June 13, 2015).

"Trustees of the Robinson Fund." Exeter, NH. Accessed July 21, 2015. exeternh.gov/bcc/trustees-robinson-fund.

Presentations/Lectures

Titcomb, Mary L. "A County Library." Paper presented at the meeting of the American Library Association, Bretton Woods, NH, June 1909.

——. "On the Trail of the Book Wagon." Paper presented at the meeting of the American Library Association, Bretton Woods, NH, June 1909.

Public Records (Census, Birth, Death, etc.)

Maryland, Hagerstown, Washington. 1910 U.S. Census, population schedule. Digital Images, Ancestry.com. Accessed February 24, 2014.

Massachusetts Vital Records, 1840–1911. Boston, Massachusetts: New England Historic Genealogical Society.

"New Hampshire Births and Christenings, 1714–1904." Index. FamilySearch, Salt Lake City, Utah, 2009, 2010. Index entries derived from digital copies of original and compiled records.

New Hampshire. Exeter. Robinson Female Seminary. Fourth Annual Catalogue: 1872–1873. Ancestry.com.

New Hampshire. Farmington, Strafford. 1850 U.S. Census, population schedule. Digital Images, Ancestry.com. Accessed February 24, 2014.

New Hampshire. Farmington, Strafford. 1860 U.S. Census, population schedule. Digital Images, Ancestry.com. Accessed February 24, 2014.

New Hampshire. Farmington, Strafford. 1870 U.S. Census, population schedule. Digital Images, Ancestry.com. Accessed February 24, 2014.

New Hampshire. Exeter, Rockingham. 1880 U.S. Census, population schedule. Digital Images, Ancestry.com. Accessed February 24, 2014.

"New Hampshire Birth Records, early to 1900." Index. FamilySearch, Salt Lake City, Utah, 2009.

New Hampshire Registrar of Vital Statistics. "Index to births, early to 1900." New Hampshire Registrar of Vital Statistics, Concord, NH.

Sleepy Hollow Cemetery Burial Record. Family plot of Dr. George E. Titcomb. Concord, MA. Deed book C, 276.

Vermont, Rutland. 1900 U.S. Census, population schedule. Digital Images, Ancestry.com. Accessed February 24, 2014.

Authored by Mary Lemist Titcomb

Titcomb, Mary L. "A County Library." Paper presented at the meeting of the American Library Association, Bretton Woods, NH, June 1909.

——. "On the Trail of the Book Wagon." Paper presented at the meeting of the American Library Association, Bretton Woods, NH, June 1909.

——. *Story of the Washington County Free Library, 1901–1931.* Hagerstown, MD: n.p., 1931.

——. "Suggestions to the Librarian of a Small Library." First Biennial Report of the Board of Library Commissioners of Vermont, 1895–96. Burlington, VT: Burlington Free Press Association, Printers, 1896.

Titcomb, Mary Lemist, and Mary Frank Mason. *Book Wagons; the County Library with Rural Book Delivery.* Chicago: American Library Association, 1922.

Titcomb, Mary Lemist, and Mary Louise Holzapfel. *The Washington County Free Library, 1901–1951* (a reissue of the *Story of the Washington County Free Library*). Hagerstown, MD: n.p., 1951.

Acknowledgments

Writing this book has been one of the great joys of my life, and, like most things joyful and worthwhile, it was not done in a vacuum. I am forever indebted to the careful and patient assistance of Jill Craig, Digitization Librarian at Western Maryland's Historical Library in Hagerstown, Maryland, who spent countless hours searching for information and archival images and sending me high-resolution copies. Jill also authored a superb article on Mary Lemist Titcomb that was published in the periodical *Catoctin History* in 2008; it is one of the most thorough, most accurate, most readable treatments of Mary Lemist Titcomb and her many accomplishments I have read. I'm also deeply grateful for the help and support of Elizabeth Howe, Reference Librarian/Certified Archivist, Washington County Free Library; Laura Schnackenberg, Bookmobile Librarian, Washington County Free Library; Darci Card, Digital Services Librarian, Utah State Library; John Gilbert Fox, photographer; and Tish Hopkins, supervisor of the Sleepy Hollow Cemetery in Concord, Massachusetts. It was a genuine pleasure to make the acquaintance of and develop friendships with two of Mary's relatives—Greata Beatty, a great-niece, and David Rodman Thomas, a great-grandnephew. They were both unfailingly gracious, helpful, and generous. Sincere thanks must also go to Kevin Plodzik, Barbara Ewen, and all the other Friends of Sleepy Hollow Cemetery who jumped on board and worked so devotedly to make sure that Mary's final resting place was properly marked and her accomplishments memorialized. I am grateful, too, to all those who contributed so willingly and so generously to the effort to raise money for the headstones of both Mary and Lydia.

To so many of my dearest friends who understood immediately why this project was so important to me and who cheered me on throughout the entire process, I say thank you from my heart. I include Melissa Dalton-Bradford, Heidi Woahn, Janie Arnold, Patricia Dudney, Geralee McArthur, MarLayne Sinclair, Sali-Kai Smith, Maggie Olsen, Kati Morton Mitchell, Janet Fotu, Barbara Langford, Lynnell Christensen, Melissa McQuarrie, and Kristi Gilbert-Ouhib, to name just a few. To the brilliant and intuitive members of my writers' group—Kristyn Crow, Danna Smith, Linda Kimball, Ken Baker, Lezlie Evans, Erin Cabatingan, Carolyn Fisher, Leah Wilcox, Trudy Harris, Kate Coombs, Polly Parkinson, Amy Finnegan, and the late Rick Walton—deepest gratitude for your insightful feedback and sustained encouragement over the years. Thanks, too, to my agent, Ronnie Herman, who immediately caught the vision of this book, and to the fabulous team at Abrams Books— my editor, Howard Reeves, Orlando Dos Reis, Masha Gunic, Amy Vreeland, Julia Marvel, Pam Notarantonio, Melissa J. Barrett, and so many others. Finally, my most profound gratitude to my husband, James, who has always been my rock and most steadfast champion and who gave me time and space and a room of my own; to my daughter, Erica, who traveled with me not only to Concord (both times), but the entire road of this journey; and to the rest of my rollicking crew of supporters—Kedric, Kelli, Kaden, Patrick, Karine, Jameson, Lizzie, Dylan, Rachel, and, last but never least, Devin. Ad infinitum!

Image Credits

Page iv: Photo courtesy of David Rodman Thomas and family. **Page 1:** (*top*) Photo courtesy of Getty OpenContent; (*bottom*) photo courtesy of David Rodman Thomas and family. **Page 2:** Public domain image. **Page 3:** 1907 postcard, owned by author. **Page 4:** (*left*) Photo courtesy of David Rodman Thomas and family; (*left*) photo courtesy of David Rodman Thomas and family. **Page 5:** Courtesy of the American Antiquarian Society. **Page 6:** (*top*) Public domain image; (*bottom*) public domain image. **Page 7:** Photo courtesy of David Rodman Thomas and family. **Page 8:** Postcard, owned by author. **Page 9:** Courtesy of Library of Congress Prints and Photographs. **Page 10:** Illustration from *Art and Architecture*. Courtesy of the Paul V. Galvin Library. **Page 11:** Public domain image. **Page 12:** Public domain image. **Page 13:** Courtesy of David Rodman Thomas and family. **Page 14:** Photo courtesy of Washington County Free Library. **Page 15:** (*top*) 1908 postcard, owned by author; (*bottom*) courtesy of Ann Newman and Suzanne Bucci. **Page 16:** Courtesy of the Washington County Free Library. **Page 18:** Courtesy of the Washington County Free Library. **Page 19:** Courtesy of the Washington County Free Library. **Page 20:** Courtesy of the Washington County Free Library. **Page 21:** Courtesy of the Washington County Free Library. **Page 22:** (*left*) Courtesy of the Washington County Free Library; (*right*) courtesy of the Washington County Free Library. **Page 23:** Photo courtesy of the Washington County Free Library. **Page 24:** Courtesy of David Rodman Thomas and family. **Page 25:** Photos courtesy of the Washington County Free Library. **Page 26:** Public domain image. **Page 27:** Photo courtesy of the Washington County Free Library. **Page 28:** (*top*) Photo courtesy of the Washington County Free Library; (*bottom*) photo courtesy of the Washington County Free Library. **Page 29:** Photo courtesy of the Washington County Free Library. **Page 30:** (*all*) Public domain images. **Page 31:** Courtesy of the Washington County Free Library. **Page 32:** Photo courtesy of the Washington County Free Library. **Page 33:** Photo courtesy of the Washington County Free Library. **Page 34:** (*left*) Photo courtesy of the Washington County Free Library; (*right*) photo courtesy of the State Library of North Carolina; (*bottom*) public domain image. **Page 35:** Photo courtesy of the Washington County Free Library. **Page 36:** Courtesy of the Washington County Free Library. **Page 37:** (*both*) Courtesy of the Washington County Free Library. **Page 38:** (*both*) Courtesy of the Washington County Free Library. **Page 39:** (*top*) Courtesy of the Washington County Free Library; (*bottom*) photo courtesy of Laura Schnackenberg, bookmobile librarian at the Washington County Free Library. **Page 42:** Photo courtesy of author. **Page 43:** Photo courtesy of the Utah State Library.

Index